GREG ELVIS

SAYULITA TRAVEL GUIDE 2024

A Comprehensive Guide to Everything You Need for an Unforgettable Sayulita Escape

Contents

1 Welcome to Sayulita   1

2 Planning Your Sayulita Escape   3

   Where is Sayulita   3

   How to Get There   4

   Visa Requirements   5

   Best Time to Visit   7

   Getting Around Sayulita   9

   Accommodations   11

   Grocery Shopping and Local Markets   16

3 Diving into the Sayulita Vibe   20

   Hitting the Waves   20

   Beyond the Beach   23

   Day Trip   27

   Immerse Yourself in Culture   31

4 10 Things to Do in Sayulita   36

5 Indulging Your Senses   43

   A Culinary Adventure   43

   Cafe and Juice Bar   46

   Nightlife Scene   48

   Shopping Spree   51

   Sustainable and Eco-Friendly Products   54

6 Practical Information   56

   Essential Sayulita   56

   Staying Connected   58

   Safety and Security Tips   61

   Additional Resources   63

Packing Essentials   67

Tour Guides Contact   69

Important Emergency Numbers and Contact Addresses   71

1

Welcome to Sayulita

As the plane descends, you excitedly look out the window, waiting for your first glimpse of Sayulita. The emerald green coast of Mexico's Riviera Nayarit stretches out below, and charming villages soon come into view.

With its colorful buildings perched atop lush hills and the turquoise Pacific Ocean lapping at its shores, Sayulita feels like a hidden gem waiting to be discovered. A wave of warmth surrounds you as you step off the plane. The tropical sun will greet you like an old friend.

The scent of salt and exotic flowers fills the air, reminding you that you have stepped away from the cares of the world and entered a world where time flows more slowly. The heartfelt hospitality of the locals will instantly make you feel at home and make you feel like you've found your second home.

The cozy warmth of the room envelops you, providing a sanctuary to rest and recharge before your adventure begins. As the sun dips below the horizon and paints the sky in shades of orange and pink, you'll be drawn to the beaches that are the heart and soul of Sayulita.

As you stroll along the shore, the soft sand soothes your feet and the rhythmic sound of the waves provides a soothing soundtrack to your thoughts. In the evening, the village comes to life with a kaleidoscope of colors and sounds.

Beach fires flicker in the darkness, casting a warm glow over the assembled crowd. As the night settles in and the sounds of the ocean lull you to sleep, you can't help but be grateful for the opportunity to experience the magic of Sayulita.

Here, surrounded by the beauty of nature and the warmth of its people, we have found a place where our sense of adventure is heightened and memories that last a lifetime are created. Welcome to Sayulita - every moment is a treasure waiting to be discovered.

2

Planning Your Sayulita Escape

Where is Sayulita

The charming seaside village of Sayulita, located on Mexico's Riviera Nayarit, enchants travelers with its laid-back atmosphere and natural beauty. Located on the Pacific Coast, Sayulita enjoys the warmth of the sun and the gentle breeze of the ocean. Traveling along the coast of western Mexico, Sayulita appears like a hidden treasure waiting to be discovered.

Located approximately 40 miles north of the vibrant city of Puerto Vallarta, Sayulita is a quiet retreat from the hustle and bustle of city life, yet accessible to travelers seeking adventure and relaxation.This village is nestled between lush hills and the clear waters of the Pacific Ocean, creating a picturesque setting that invites exploration.

Sayulita's laid-back charm and vibrant culture have earned it a reputation as a haven for surfers, artists, and travelers seeking an authentic Mexican experience. Sayulita is located on the Riviera Nayarit and offers the perfect balance of peace and excitement.

Surrounded by lush tropical vegetation and overlooking the sparkling waters of Banderas Bay, Sayulita offers a tranquil retreat for those seeking relaxation and rejuvenation. Still, its proximity to Puerto Vallarta allows visitors to enjoy the quiet life of the village while still having easy access to the amenities and attractions of the big city.

How to Get There

Puerto Vallarta International Airport (PVR): The most direct route to paradise. Once you land, take advantage of our convenient shuttle, taxi, or private car service. Surrounded by swaying palm trees and turquoise waters, this scenic coastal cruise lasts approximately 45 minutes and lets you soak in the beauty that awaits.

By Air

Consider Guadalajara International Airport (GDL). Although the itinerary is long (approximately 5-6 hours by bus), the winding roads reveal hidden gems of Mexico's countryside and quaint towns. Budget-friendly and packed with local flavor, this option is perfect for those looking for an authentic experience.

By Bus

For budget-minded travelers, several bus companies offer direct routes from major cities such as Guadalajara and Mazatlan. The journey takes about 7-8 hours, but you can't beat the affordability and local experience. Enjoy snacks and entertainment, and experience the rhythm of Mexican life from the train window.

Tips for a Smooth Landing

- Booking your transportation in advance will ensure a stress-free arrival, especially during high season.
- Find the lowest prices on flights, buses and shuttles.
- Think of your travel time as part of your adventure.
- Enjoy your Sayulita vacation by taking in the sights, sounds, and local culture.

Remember, your trip to Sayulita is just the beginning. The excitement builds with every step you take, and this sun-drenched oasis promises an unforgettable experience. Pack your bags, choose your adventure, and fall in love with the magic of Sayulita!

Visa Requirements

For travelers planning a visit to Sayulita, Mexico, it's important to understand visa requirements and immigration procedures to ensure a smooth and hassle-free trip. Here's a comprehensive guide to help you navigate the process: Visa requirements:

Tourist visa (FMM)

Many countries including the United States, Canada, European Union, Australia, and Japan If you are entering Mexico as a national tourist, you do not need a visa. Instead, visitors are typically issued a tourist visa, known as a Forma Migratoria Multiple (FMM), upon arrival at a port of entry.

FMM allows tourists to stay in Mexico for up to 180 days (approximately 6 months) for leisure and recreational activities. It is important to note that FMM does not permit visitors to engage in paid work or business activities while in Mexico.

Visitor Visa (Visitante)

Nationals of some countries may require a Visitor Visa (Visitante) to enter Mexico, depending on their nationality and the purpose of their visit. A tourist visa is typically required for travelers planning a long-term stay in Mexico or traveling for a specific purpose, such as study abroad, work, or a family reunion.

The requirements for obtaining a tourist visa vary depending on the nationality of the traveler and the specific circumstances of the visit.

Entry Procedures

Passport Expiration Date: All visitors to Mexico, regardless of nationality, must present a valid passport upon entry. Your passport must be valid for at least 6 months beyond your intended stay in Mexico.

Tourist Card (FMM): When travelers arrive in Mexico, they receive a Tourist Card (FMM) from the immigration office at the port of entry.FMM must be completed and submitted along with associated fees.The fee is usually included in the ticket price or paid at the airport.FMM must be kept during your stay in Mexico and returned upon departure.

Customs Declaration Form: Travelers entering Mexico must complete a customs declaration form to declare goods and valuables being imported into the country. It is important to accurately declare all items subject to customs regulations, such as cash, electronics, alcohol, and tobacco products.

Health Declaration: Due to public health concerns, especially during times of heightened health alert or pandemic, travelers may be required to complete a health declaration form upon entering Mexico. Health declaration forms typically include questions about recent travel history, symptoms of illness, and possible exposure to infectious diseases.

Additional Requirements: Depending on your country of origin and the specific circumstances of your visit, you may be required to provide additional documentation or meet specific entry requirements established by Mexican immigration authorities.

Before planning your trip, we recommend that you review the latest travel advisories and entry requirements for Mexico and ensure that all relevant regulations are complied with.

Best Time to Visit

Choosing the best time to visit Sayulita is like choosing the most vivid brush-strokes of a masterpiece, setting the tone for the entire experience.Sayulita enjoys a wonderful tropical climate year-round. However, if you know the season, crowds, and weather conditions, you can tailor your visit to your preferences.

Season

High season (November to April)

Sayulita's high season coincides with the dry season, bringing clear skies and mild temperatures, making it ideal for relaxing on the beach and outdoor activities Perfect for enjoying.

At this time of year, there is an influx of tourists escaping the cold weather, resulting in the entire village turning into busy streets and a vibrant energy. Demand for accommodation and activities may increase during this period. Therefore, we recommend booking in advance to secure your spot.

Low Season (May-June, October): Sayulita's low season offers the perfect balance between fewer crowds and a pleasant climate. May and June are the transition period from the dry season to the rainy season, with occasional afternoon showers easing the heat. In October, the rainy season ends, and the scenery becomes lush and green after the rain.

Low season (July to September): Sayulita's low season coincides with the rainy season, which is characterized by daily tropical rain and high humidity. While rain may deter some from traveling, the off-season offers budget-conscious travelers the opportunity to enjoy discounted rates on accommodations and activities.

Despite the rain, Sayulita retains its laid-back charm, and adventurous travelers can enjoy outdoor adventures in between rain showers.

Crowds

Sayulita sees the most tourists during peak seasons, especially during major holidays and festivals. Weekends tend to be busier than weekdays, with locals and day trippers from surrounding towns flocking to the village to enjoy the beach and lively atmosphere.

To avoid the crowds, visit Sayulita during the off-season or off-season when there are fewer tourists and a more relaxing experience.

Weather

Sayulita enjoys a tropical climate with mild temperatures and abundant sunshine year-round. The dry season from November to April is characterized by sunny skies and daytime temperatures of 24–32 °C.

The rainy season, from May to October, brings occasional afternoon showers and high humidity with temperatures in the mid-70s to low-80s (24–31 degrees). Even during the rainy season, mornings often begin to clear, making it the perfect time to do some outdoor activities before the afternoon rain sets in.

In summary, the best time to visit Sayulita depends on the weather, crowds, and budget preferences. Whether you prefer the vibrant energy of high season or the tranquility of low season, Sayulita welcomes you with open arms all year round for an unforgettable and enchanting experience

Getting Around Sayulita

Traveling around Sayulita is a great adventure in itself, with a variety of transportation options to suit different tastes and lifestyles. Whether you prefer leisurely walking, freecycling, or the convenience of a taxi or golf cart, exploring Sayulita's charming streets and beautiful surroundings is easy.

Walking

Sayulita's compact size and pedestrian-friendly streets make walking the preferred mode of transportation for many visitors. Stroll through the Village and soak up the lively atmosphere, admire the colorful murals, and discover hidden treasures around every corner.

Walking gives you the flexibility to explore the area at your own pace, including hitting the beach, browsing local shops, and sampling street food.

Cycling

Cycling is a popular way to explore Sayulita and the surrounding area, and is a fun and environmentally friendly alternative to hiking. Sayulita's several rental shops offer bikes for daily or hourly rates, making it easy to explore the village streets and scenic coastal trails.

Taxi

Taxis are readily available in Sayulita and are a convenient mode of transportation, especially for long distances or people with disabilities. Taxis can be found at designated stops within the village, but they can also be picked up on the street.

Fares are usually negotiated with the driver before the trip begins. Therefore, we recommend that you check the prices in advance to avoid misunderstandings.

Golf Cart

Golf carts are Sayulita's favorite and iconic means of transportation, allowing you to explore the village and surrounding area in fun and style. Many rental agencies in Sayulita offer golf cart rentals for daily or weekly rentals, so you can get around in comfort and style. The golf cart is especially useful for accessing secluded beaches and exploring nearby attractions outside the village center.

ATVs and Scooters

If you're looking for a more adventurous mode of transportation, you can rent ATVs and scooters in Sayulita. These motorized vehicles provide access to off-road trails and remote beaches not accessible by other modes of transportation. When riding an ATV or scooter in Sayulita, it is important to wear proper safety equipment and obey local traffic laws.

Accommodations

Finding the Perfect Place to Stay

Hotel

Casa Karma Hotel Boutique

Address: Calle Marlin #16, Sayulita, Nayarit, Mexico.

This luxurious boutique hotel offers stunning sea views, an infinity pool, and an on-site spa, perfect for those seeking the ultimate in relaxation and luxury. Perched on a cliff overlooking North Beach, it offers breathtaking panoramas and direct access to the waves.

Hotelito Mio

Address: Av Revolución #19, Sayulita, Nayarit, Mexico.

This charming and colorful hotel combines Mexican tradition with modern facilities. With lively rooms, a roof terrace with sea views and a central location, our hotel is ideal for those seeking a balance between comfort and cultural immersion.

La Bahia Luxury Suites & Residences

Address: Av.Del Palmer #48, Sayulita, Nayarit, Mexico.

This luxury hotel offers spacious suites and residences with private balconies or terraces, many with sea views. It features a swim-up bar, an infinity pool and a restaurant serving delicious local cuisine. Located on the quiet southern tip of Sayulita, it's perfect for families and those seeking a quiet retreat.

Boutique Hotel

Amor Boutique Hotel

Address: Pescadores S/N, Sayulita, Nayarit, Mexico

Located on a quiet street near North Beach, this hotel offers a bohemian atmosphere with elegant rooms, yoga classes, and surfboard rentals. Enjoy sea views from the pool and enjoy fresh seafood at the restaurant.

Hotel Boutique Siete Lunas

Address: Camino a Playa Los Muertos 714 3a sección 63734, Sayulita, Nayarit, Mexico

Perched on a hill overlooking the city, this luxurious hotel offers sea-facing bungalows with private terraces and plunge pools.

Hostel

Selina Sayulita

Address: Calle Gaviota #12, Sayulita, Nayarit, Mexico.

This lively hostel offers a variety of dorms, private rooms and a rooftop . Pool, bar and restaurant. With its social atmosphere, events and activities, it's perfect for solo travelers or groups looking to socialize.

Viajero Sayulita

Address: Calle Primavera #16, between Av Naranjito and Av Revolución, Sayulita, Nayarit, Mexico.

This adults-only hostel offers a trendy atmosphere with stylish dorms and private rooms, a rooftop pool with stunning views, and a bar and restaurant. Offering yoga classes, surfing lessons, and other activities, it's perfect for active and sociable travelers.

My Sisters House

Address: Av Revolución #16, Sayulita, Nayarit, Mexico.

This women-only hostel provides a safe and supportive environment for female travelers. It offers dormitory and private rooms, a shared kitchen and a rooftop terrace with sea views.

Budget-Friendly Options

Almar Sayulita

Address: Av.Delfín #8, Sayulita, Nayarit, Mexico

This eco-friendly hostel offers dorms and private rooms with a focus on sustainability. Relax in a hammock, enjoy a healthy meal at the cafe, or take part in a beach cleanup or yoga class. Perfect for budget-friendly and environmentally conscious travelers.

La Patrona Hostel & Bar

Address: Av Revolución #9, Sayulita, Nayarit, Mexico

This lively hostel offers a sociable atmosphere with a bar, a rooftop terrace with sea views, and a pool table We offer Offering surfing lessons, bike rentals, and other activities, it's perfect for travelers on a budget looking for adventure and connection.

Family Stay

Hotel Don Olas

Address: Av Revolución #60, Sayulita, Nayarit, Mexico

This beachfront hotel is spacious with a balcony or terrace, perfect for families. Children will love the on-site pool, playground and surfing school. Enjoy delicious Mexican cuisine at the restaurant or relax with a massage by the sea.

Airbnb and Vacation

Casa Tranquila Oceanfront Paradise

Location: Located on the north end of Sayulita, steps from the beach and popular surf spots.

Enjoy the beachfront atmosphere with a stay in this stunning 4-bedroom villa. Featuring a private pool, hot tub, and direct beach access, this rental is perfect for families and groups looking for the ultimate in relaxation.

Enjoy breathtaking ocean views, cook delicious meals in the gourmet kitchen, and relax in the hammock garden.

Casa Mandara Oceanfront Retreat

Location: Located on the quiet southern tip of Sayulita, this hotel offers a peaceful retreat with easy access to the beach.

Experience luxurious beachfront living in this 5-bedroom villa. With breathtaking ocean views, a private infinity pool, and a rooftop terrace with a hot tub, this rental is perfect for those looking for an unforgettable vacation. Relax on the sun loungers, enjoy a yoga session on the terrace or enjoy a chef-prepared meal.

Grocery Shopping and Local Markets

Sayulita, Mexico is more than just surfing and sunsets. There's also a vibrant dining scene, featuring fresh local produce and delicious produce. Whether you're cooking up a feast in your vacation rental or buying a quick snack, here's a guide to grocery shopping in Sayulita and local markets:

Supermarket

Don Rodolfo: Food Essentials such as wine, snacks, and household items. Conveniently located across from Trancos on the main road.

Sayulita Market: Located near North Beach, this deli specializes in prepared foods, breads, pastries, and gourmet foods. Perfect for stocking up on delicious picnic essentials and prepared meals.

La Comer Bucerías: For a larger selection and wider aisles, head to nearby Bucerías (10-minute drive).This supermarket stocks everything from fresh produce to international brands.

Local Market

Sayulita Farmers Market (Mercado del Pueblo): Open Fridays from 10 am to 2 pm (November to April), this lively market sells fresh fruits and vegetables, locally grown Cheeses, baked goods and crafts made with and more. Soak up the lively atmosphere and support local providers.

Tianguis: This outdoor market takes place on Sundays on Gaviotas Street and features stalls selling clothing, jewelry, crafts, and local food. Haggling is encouraged and enriches the cultural experience.

Fish Market: Located near the Main Street Bridge, this market features fresh seafood caught daily. Choose your fish and a local vendor will prepare it for you. A must-see for seafood lovers.

Organic and Specialty Foods: Sayulita Organic and Sayulita Life offer organic products, healthy snacks, and specialty foods for those looking for specialized nutritional options.

Street Vendors: Street vendors can be found throughout the city selling fruits, vegetables, snacks, and local delicacies like churros and coconut water. Perfect for a quick and refreshing meal.

Shopping Tips

Carry Reusable Bags: Many stores, markets, and vendors are charging for plastic bags.

Bring cash: Small stores and merchants may not accept cards.

Polish your Spanish: Simple phrases can help you communicate and even help you negotiate prices.

Enjoy the experience: Take time to explore the market, chat with vendors, and sample local produce. Who knows, you might even find some hidden treasure or unique ingredient.

Access to medical facilities and pharmacies is very important to travelers visiting Sayulita.Although it is a small village, there are several options for purchasing medical care and medicines.

Here is a guide to medical care and pharmacy in Sayulita:

Clinics

Sayulita Red Cross (Cruz Roja): The Sayulita Red Cross provides emergency medical services and first aid to residents and visitors.They offer a Red Cross Clinic located in the heart of Sayulita and train medical professionals who can provide basic medical care and stabilization in emergencies. For more serious illnesses, the clinic also provides referrals to nearby hospitals and specialists.

Private Clinics

Sayulita has several private clinics that provide a wide range of medical services, including general consultations, emergency care, laboratory tests, and minor procedures. These clinics may be staffed by bilingual medical professionals and equipped with the latest medical equipment and equipment.

Pharmacy

Pharmacias Guadalajara

Pharmacias Guadalajara is a well-known Mexican pharmacy chain with a convenient branch in Sayulita. This pharmacy carries a wide selection of prescription and over-the-counter medications, as well as personal care products, vitamins, medications, and more.

Local Pharmacies

In addition to Pharmacies in Guadalajara, Sayulita has several independent pharmacies and drugstores. These pharmacies sell a variety of medicines and health products, including prescription drugs, over-the-counter medicines, and herbal supplements. Pharmacists at these facilities may be able to provide advice and support in choosing appropriate medications for minor illnesses.

Travel Insurance

We recommend that travelers visiting Sayulita purchase travel insurance that includes coverage for medical emergencies and evacuations. Travel Insurance provides peace of mind and financial protection in the event of unexpected illness, injury, or treatment during your trip.

Precautions

Healthcare in Sayulita is generally of high quality, but it is important to take precautions to stay healthy during your visit. Drink bottled water to avoid water-borne illnesses and maintain good hygiene, including washing your hands frequently.

Use sunscreen and protective clothing to prevent sunburn and heat-related illnesses, and avoid mosquito bites to reduce the risk of mosquito-borne illnesses.

Familiarizing yourself with Sayulita's medical options and pharmacies will give you peace of mind knowing that medical assistance or medication is always available should you need it during your visit to this tropical paradise.

3

Diving into the Sayulita Vibe

Hitting the Waves

Surfing, stand-up paddleboarding (SUP), kayaking, snorkeling, diving, and boat tours are popular water activities in Sayulita, giving travelers the chance to explore beautiful coastal scenery and a vibrant marine ecosystem.ures in Sayulita:

Surfing

Lessons

Sayulita has excellent surfing, with waves suitables of surfers, from beginners to experienced surfers. It is known for its surfing environment.

Many surfing schools and instructors offer lessons and surfboard rentals for those looking to learn and improve their skills.

Beginners can start in the calmer waves near the shore, while experienced surfers can venture into nearby waves for more challenging rides.

Best Surf Spots

Sayulita Beach: Sayulita's main beach offers consistent waves and a lively atmosphere, perfect for beginner and intermediate surfers.

Playa Los Muertos: Located a short distance south of Sayulita, Playa Los Muertos offers beautiful views and uncrowded waves, perfect for experienced surfers looking for a quiet spot.

Punta Mita: Just a short drive from Sayulita, Punta Mita is home to world-class surf spots like La Rancha and El Anclote, and attracts experienced surfers looking for bigger waves and epic rides.

Stand Up Paddleboard (SUP), Kayak, and Boat Tours

SUP and Kayak

Sayulita's tranquil coves and crystal clear waters are perfect for stand up paddleboarding and kayaking adventures.

Rent equipment at a local rental shop or take a guided tour to explore the coast, paddle through mangrove estuaries, and discover hidden beaches and coves.

Stand Up Paddleboards and Kayaks are a great option for all ages and skill levels to experience the beauty of the Sayulita Coast in a fun and scenic way.

Boat Tours

Boat tours are a great way to explore the Sayulita coast and nearby attractions, including secluded beaches, hidden caves, and offshore islands.

Take a guided boat tour and experience activities like whale watching, dolphin encounters, snorkeling, and sunset cruises.

Local Tour Operator offers a variety of boat tours, from small group trips to private charters, so you can customize your experience to suit your needs.

Snorkeling and Diving

Snorkeling

Sayulita's crystal clear waters are rich in marine life, and snorkeling is a popular activity for visitors. Join a guided snorkeling tour to explore colorful coral reefs, swim with colorful fish, and encounter sea turtles, rays, octopuses, and other marine life. Several travel companies offer snorkeling tours to nearby snorkeling spots, such as Marietas Islands and Los Arcos Marine Park.

Diving

For certified divers, Sayulita offers access to some of Mexico's most spectacular dive sites, including underwater caves, reefs, and offshore sea stacks. Sayulita's dive operators organize guided dives to explore underwater ecosystems, observe marine wildlife.

Beyond the Beach

Hike the Sayulita Jungle

Enter a realm where the vibrant heartbeat of nature pulsates through the leaves and the chirping of birds. The jungles of Sayulita beckon with lush greenery, winding roads, and hidden wonders waiting to be discovered by intrepid explorers.

As you step onto the forest floor, the scent of exotic flowers fills the air and the sound of a roaring waterfall echoes in the distance. Hiking trails wind through dense vegetation, offering glimpses of towering palm trees, towering ferns, and vibrant orchids clinging to moss-covered rocks.

Every step brings you closer to the heartbeat of the jungle. There, every nook and cranny is teeming with life and dappled sunlight filters through the forest canopy. Seek advice from an experienced guide or venture out on your own and you'll encounter natural wonders along the way.

Discover hidden waterfalls that flow into crystal clear pools where you can cool off with a refreshing swim amidst the sound of water and the chirping of birds. The higher you climb, the more panoramic views open up, taking in the surrounding mountains, the jungle canopy, and the sparkling ocean beyond.

Stop, catch your breath, and enjoy the beauty of the landscape unfolding before you, a testament to the wild majesty of nature. As you hike, become aware of the rich life that surrounds you.

Listen to howler monkeys chirp in the trees, spot colorful butterflies flitting through the leaves, and marvel at the intricate patterns of sunlight dancing on the forest floor. Whether you're looking for adventure, solitude, or a deeper connection with nature, hiking in the Sayulita Jungle provides an unforgettable experience that will leave you feeling empowered, inspired, and in awe of nature.

Yoga Studio and Wellness Retreat

Sayulita's yoga studio and wellness retreat offers a sanctuary for self-discovery and holistic healing, where the rhythms of the ocean and whispers of the wind create a harmonious backdrop for wellness practices.

Enter a world of tranquility as you enter our yoga studio, decorated with colorful tapestries, flickering candles, and the gentle scent of incense.

Here, experienced instructors guide practitioners of all levels through a journey of movement, breath, and mindfulness, promoting a sense of balance, strength, and inner peace.classes range from dynamic vinyasa flows to restorative yin sessions, each tailored to the needs of body, mind, and spirit.

Whether you want to increase strength and flexibility, relieve tension and stress, or simply connect with yourself, Sayulita Yoga Studio offers a sanctuary that nourishes your body, mind, and soul.

Outside the studio, Sayulita has a vibrant community of wellness practitioners and holistic healers, offering a variety of services and treatments to support your journey to health. From massage therapy and energy healing to sound baths and herbal medicine, Sayulita's wellness products offer a holistic approach to health and healing that addresses the needs of the whole person.

Zipline in Sayulita

Imagine soaring high above the green canopy of Sayulita's lush jungle, the wind rushing from tree to tree as it blows past your face. Ziplining in Sayulita offers a thrilling adventure that combines adrenaline-pumping excitement with breathtaking views of the surrounding landscape.

Sayulita offers several zipline tours that take you on an exhilarating journey through the treetops and offer panoramic views of the jungle, mountains, and ocean beyond. The popular zipline spot is a short drive from Sayulita and features a series of platforms connected by ziplines across the canopy.

When you glide effortlessly through the air, you can feel a sense of freedom and exhilaration like no other. For an unforgettable zipline experience, head to Canopy River in nearby Puerto Vallarta City.

Here you can take a canopy tour that includes a network of ziplines, suspension bridges, and rappel lines set against the backdrop of the Sierra Madre Mountains. As you travel your route, keep an eye out for local wildlife such as tropical birds, monkeys, and iguanas.

After your zipline adventure, relax at one of Sayulita's many charming cafes and beachfront restaurants, enjoy a delicious meal, and soak up the relaxed atmosphere of this vibrant coastal town.

Sayulita ATV Adventure

Rev up your engine and get ready to explore the rugged terrain around Sayulita on an adrenaline-pumping ATV adventure. Sayulita offers plenty of opportunities to explore off-road, with winding trails, beautiful scenery, and hidden gems waiting to be discovered.

Sayulita's popular ATV adventure takes you through the jungle to the nearby village of San Pancho. There we cross riverbeds, climb steep hills, and splash through muddy puddles to reach the beach.

Along the way, you'll enjoy breathtaking views of the coastline and lush countryside, and there will be plenty of opportunities to stop and photograph the stunning scenery. For a more challenging ATV adventure, head inland to the Sierra Madre Mountains.

There, rugged roads wind through dense forests and rugged terrain. Here you'll navigate rocky paths, cross shallow rivers, and climb to dizzying heights while enjoying panoramic views of the surrounding countryside.

After a day on your ATV, take a refreshing dip in the ocean or treat yourself to a relaxing massage at Sayulita's Wellness Spa to relax and recharge after an exciting outdoor excursion.

Sayulita Eco Tour

Discover the natural beauty and rich biodiversity of Sayulita's pristine ecosystem on an eco-tour that provides a deeper understanding of local flora and fauna and conservation efforts.

Sayulita offers a variety of eco-tours that will take you to the heart of secluded nature, where you can explore mangrove estuaries, lush jungles, and pristine beaches. Sayulita's popular eco-tour takes you on a guided hike through the jungle to a secluded waterfall.

There you can swim in the crystal clear sea and cool off from the tropical heat. Along the way, your guide will introduce you to local flora and fauna and explain about the local ecosystem and the importance of nature conservation.

Another eco-friendly activity at Sayulita is sea turtle conservation. Here you can take guided tours to observe nesting turtles and learn about conservation efforts for these endangered species. During the breeding season, volunteers patrol the coast at night to monitor turtle activity and ensure the safety of nesting females and their eggs.

Day Trip

Sayulita's charming atmosphere and captivating landscape make it the perfect base from which to explore the surrounding wonders of Riviera Nayarit. From pristine beaches to picturesque villages, there are many destinations to explore.

Here's a guide to some of the most fascinating day trips from Sayulita:

Punta Mita

Known for its world-class luxury accommodations, just a short drive from Sayulita There is the luxury resort town of Punta Mita.

Take a day trip to Punta Mita, relax on the exclusive beach of Playa Punta de Mita, enjoy a gourmet meal at a beachside restaurant, or take a snorkeling tour to the nearby Marietas Islands. Punta Mita also offers surfing, paddling, and whale watching during the winter months.

Directions

By Car

Rent a car or taxi and take a scenic drive along the coast to Punta Mita.

Depending on traffic, the trip takes between 30 and 45 minutes.

By Shuttle

Many travel companies in Sayulita offer shuttle services to Punta Mita, providing convenient transportation for day-trippers.

San Pancho (San Francisco)

Experience the laid-back charm of San Pancho, a quaint seaside village known for its artistic community, pristine beaches, and tranquil atmosphere. Stroll through the colorful streets lined with boutiques and galleries, relax on the golden sands of Playa San Pancho, or enjoy fresh seafood at the beachfront Palapa Restaurant.

San Pancho also offers horseback riding, bird watching, and exploring nearby nature preserves.

Directions

By Car: Drive or taxi to San Pancho, about 15-20 minutes north of Sayulita on Highway 200.

By Bike: Rent a Bike and Cycle the Trail Enjoy panoramic views of the Pacific Ocean as you ride the scenic coastal road to San Pancho.

Sayulita's Surrounding Beaches

Beyond Sayulita's main beach, discover Riviera Nayarit's hidden treasures, including secluded coves, pristine coves, and unspoiled coastline.

Explore the golden sands of Playa de los Muertos, snorkel in the turquoise waters of Playa Calixitos, or soak up the sun on the tranquil shores of Playa Patzcuarito. Each beach has its own charm and offers opportunities for relaxation and adventure.

Directions

Walking: Many of the beaches around Sayulita are accessible via beautiful hiking trails or along the coastline from the main beach.

By Boat: Rent a local boat or join a guided tour to explore secluded beaches and hidden coves along the coast, free to swim, snorkel, and sunbathe in unspoiled nature.

Marietas Islands

The Marietas Islands are a protected marine reserve known for their amazing biodiversity and famous hidden beach, Playa del Amor (Hidden Beach). Explore the islands' volcanic rock formations, snorkel among colorful coral reefs, and admire diverse marine life including dolphins, manta rays, and sea turtles.

Don't miss the opportunity to visit Playa del Amor. It can only be accessed by swimming or kayaking through natural tunnels between the rocks.

Directions

By Boat Tour: Join a guided boat tour departing from Sayulita or nearby Punta Mita. This tour includes round-trip transportation to Marietas Islands, as well as snorkeling, swimming, and exploring hidden beaches.

Many tour operators provide snorkeling equipment, kayaks, and knowledgeable guides to enhance your experience.

Vallarta Botanical Gardens

Step into the vibrant world of flora and fauna at the Vallarta Botanical Gardens, a nature lover's paradise. Hike through the jungle on varied trails, see more than 3,000 plant species, and watch for rare birds flitting through the trees.

Take a dip in a hidden waterfall, refresh yourself in an orchid house, and reconnect with nature in this tranquil paradise.

Directions

The gardens are about a 40-minute drive from Sayulita. You can rent a car, or taxi, or take a guided tour that includes transportation.

Canopy River Expedition

Get your adrenaline pumping with an unforgettable Canopy River Expedition. Zipline through a lush rainforest canopy, rappel down waterfalls and float down crystal-clear rivers on this action-packed adventure.

Directions

Most Canopy River expedition companies offer transportation from your Sayulita accommodation, making it a hassle-free experience.

Altamira Ruins

Step back in time and explore the ancient Altamira Ruins, the remains of a pre-Hispanic city dating back more than 1,000 years. Trek through the jungle to reach ruins, marvel at intricate stone structures and imagine the lives of the people who once lived on this land.

Directions

The Altamira ruins are about an hour's drive from Sayulita. We recommend renting a car or joining a guided tour with transportation.

Bonus Tip: Whichever day trip you choose, remember to pack comfortable shoes, sunscreen, bug repellent, and a reusable water bottle to stay hydrated and eco-friendly.

Most importantly, embrace the spirit of adventure, connect with local culture, and create unforgettable memories in the heart of Riviera Nayarit.

Immerse Yourself in Culture

Art Galleries, Boutiques, and Local Crafts

Location: Sayulita's vibrant arts and crafts scene spans the town's charming streets. Numerous galleries, boutiques, and craft stores line the colorful buildings and lush vegetation.

Art Gallery

Stroll through the cobblestone streets of Sayulita and you'll come across numerous art galleries showcasing the work of talented local and international artists.

These galleries are located in different parts of the city and offer a wide range of art styles, from traditional Mexican painting to modern sculpture.

Near the main square, Galeria Tanana features impressive works inspired by the region's natural beauty. Another must-visit is Colectika, located on Calle Delfín,

Boutiques

Sayulita's boutiques exude bohemian charm, with each store having its own unique style and personality. They can be found all over the city's busy streets, displaying a wide variety of clothing, accessories, and household items.

Stroll down Calle Revolucion and you'll find exquisite boutiques like Evoke the Spirit, known for its handmade jewelry and bohemian-chic clothing.

Local Crafts

For a taste of authentic Mexican craftsmanship, visit Sayulita's local craft stores. There are many handmade treasures made by skilled craftsmen. These shops are scattered throughout the city and offer everything from intricately woven textiles to hand-painted pottery.

Visit Artefakto, on Calle Jose Mariscal to browse an impressive collection of locally made ceramics, textiles, and home accessories. Nearby, at Mexi Arte, you'll find a colorful array of Mexican handicrafts, including Huichol beadwork and Oaxacan alebrijes.

Sayulita Farmers Market

Fresh Produce and Crafts

Location: The Sayulita Farmers Market is held every Friday from 10 a.m. to 2 p.m. in Plaza Pueblito, the city's main square. This lively square is close to the city center and is easily accessible from anywhere in Sayulita.

Fresh Food

As you enter Plaza Pueblito, you are greeted by the vibrant sights and aromas of the Sayulita Farmers Market. Lined with colorful stalls, you'll find fresh fruit, vegetables, and herbs sourced directly from local farmers and producers.

Enjoy juicy mangoes, ripe avocados, and fragrant basil, or try exotic fruits like dragon fruit and papaya. At the market, each stall offers an attractive selection of seasonal products to stimulate your senses.

Artisan Goods

In addition to fresh produce, the Sayulita Farmers Market is a treasure trove of crafts made by local artisans. Browse stalls filled with handmade jewelry, textiles, and artwork.

Each piece reflects the unique style and creativity of its creator. From intricately woven baskets to hand-painted pottery, there's something on the market to suit every taste and budget.

Street Food and Snacks

Hungry shoppers can indulge in a variety of street food and snacks at the market. Sample delicious tacos, tamales, and empanadas made by local vendors, or satisfy your sweet tooth with freshly baked pastries and desserts.

Don't miss the opportunity to taste traditional Mexican dishes such as elote (grilled corn) and churros, paired with refreshing agua fresca or freshly squeezed juice.

Live Music and Entertainment

Adding to the festive atmosphere of the Market, live musicians and artists entertain visitors with traditional music, dance, and cultural performances. Take a break from shopping, enjoy lively music and energetic dance performances, and soak up the vibrant spirit of Sayulita's local community.

Traditional Dance Performances and Cultural Events

Location: Traditional dance performances and cultural events are held at various locations in Sayulita, including the town's main square, local theaters, and cultural centers.

Main Square

Sayulita's main square, Plaza Pueblito, serves as the stage for many traditional dance performances and cultural events throughout the year. Visitors can gather in the plaza's shaded seating areas to watch local dance groups perform traditional dances such as the Jarave Tapatio (Mexican Hat Dance) and the Danza de los Viezitos (Old Man's Dance).

These vibrant performances often feature colorful costumes, energetic music, and elaborate choreography, offering a glimpse into Mexico's rich cultural heritage.

Local Theaters and Cultural Centers

In addition to performances in the main square, Sayulita has several theaters and cultural centers that host traditional dance performances, musical concerts, and cultural events.

Look for events at venues like Sayulita Cultural Center on Calle Revolución. A diverse cultural program is offered, including dance workshops, art exhibitions, and live performances showcasing the talents of local artists and artists.

4

10 Things to Do in Sayulita

Although Sayulita is small, there is plenty to do in this charming little town. To get the most out of your stay and Sayulita activities, you should stay at least two full days. However, we highly recommend booking for at least 4 days to get the most out of it.

Spend Time on the Beach

One of the best things to do in Sayulita is to make the most of the beach. After all, this is the blissful Riviera Nayarit, with the Pacific Ocean stretching out before you. There are four main beaches near Sayulita, including the town beach (Playa Sayulita), which tends to be the busiest.

Sayulita's best beaches are just outside of town but within walking distance. Most beaches have restaurants/beach bars or beach clubs where you can drink and eat, in addition to lounge chairs and umbrellas.

If you'd like to bring your own drinks or picnic and lay out on a towel in the sand, there are plenty of options for that too.

Many of Sayulita's beaches are not suitable for swimming, as they have waves that are suitable for surfing but not for swimming. The waves are high and the current is strong. If you want to swim, be sure to head to Los Muertos Beach, where the waves are calmest and there is a designated swimming area.

The best beaches are:

Playa Escondida/Carricitos – Great beach to enjoy the sunset,There is a restaurant, but overall it is a pretty pristine beach. Be sure to bring snacks and drinks for your sunset picnic.

Los Muertos Beach, near Punta Sayulita - A small bay beach lined with palm trees, with yellow sand and turquoise water. Best beaches for swimming in Sayulita. It has two bars that sell drinks and simple Mexican food.

Playa Malpaso near San Pancho – For a secluded and wild experience, hike from the north end of Sayulita Beach across the headland to the end at Malpaso Beach. It's an adventure in itself and you get pristine beaches with no infrastructure. There is really only pure nature here. It is also accessible by taxi or San Pancho.

Go Boutique Shopping

Sayulita is a great place to shop for unique boutique and local products. As you explore, you'll find all the beautiful boutiques. Most of the pieces on display are locally made, many by local Jalisco designers, combining local culture, history, and tradition.

San Pancho's Concept Store Sayulita features a wide range of boutiques, including shops selling jewelry, clothing, art, home accessories, swimwear, and surfwear.

Evoke the Spirit - A beautiful and unique concept store selling clothing, unique jewelry, and home decor. Evoke the Spirit was created by Britney Borgeson, a New Yorker who has called Sayulita his home for the past 10 years.

The piece you see was designed by Britney and made by local Huichol artisans. It beautifully combines Huichol tradition with modern design and taste.

Revolucion del Sueno – A colorful boutique selling unique prints, bags, and other beautiful décor and home goods.

Artefakto – Beautiful works from various artistic communities across Mexico. There's a lot of art to see here, including homewares, bags, hammocks, and more. This is a great way to support local communities across the country.

Manyana – A stunning home decor and clothing boutique with minimalist style and Japanese aesthetics. Beautiful pottery and clothing.

En Plural Concept Store – Unique clothing designs from local Guadalajaran designers. There is a larger store in San Pancho that also sells art prints.

Zafiro – Beautiful jewelry with many precious stones.

SayulitaSol - Beautiful Gold and Silver Plated Handcrafted Jewelry

Go Surfing

Mexico's Pacific Coast offers some of the best surfing in the Americas, especially for beginners and intermediate surfers. The beach and tides here provide plenty of white water for beginner surfers, and consistent waves for those who have already spent some time on a board.

Near Sayulita's main beach, there are many small surf shops and schools where you can take surfing lessons. You can also rent boards at the same surfing school. Group lessons, private lessons, and rentals are easy to find in Sayulita. Some of the best surfing schools in the city include Lunazul, Marea, and Avex Surf.

Go Whale Watching

If you're in Mexico during whale watching season, don't miss the opportunity to go whale watching, especially if you've never been to Mexico before.

Whale Watching

The whale watching season in Mexico is very short and only lasts from December to March each year, but during this period you are almost guaranteed to see humpback whales in Banderas Bay.

To see whales, you'll need to take a boat ride as part of a tour or rent a luxury boat for a day trip on the water. We recommend doing your research before contacting a travel agent. You need to find a captain who cares about the whales and knows how to approach them without spooking them.

Watch the sunset at Carricitos Beach

One of the best beaches in Sayulita is Carricitos Beach. It is located on the opposite side of the promontory west of the town of Sayulita. Playa Carricitos

Sayulita is about 20-minute walk from the town of Sayulita, but the road is a bit uphill. It is accessible by motorcycle, ATV, and golf cart, but the narrow roads make it a little more difficult by car.

Carricitos Beach is perfect for watching the sun set over the ocean (facing due west). The beach is still quite pristine. It is the only accommodation and restaurant located directly on the beach, the rest is overgrown with plants and palm trees.

After all, it can be said to be Sayulita's hidden beach,There's not much to buy here, so bring all your snacks and drinks and come watch the sunset. A perfect end to a beautiful day in Sayulita.

Go Horseback Riding

Enjoying the beach on horseback is a refreshing change from just taking a walk. Go on a local adventure on horseback through the villages, jungles, and beautiful beaches of Higuera Blanca.

Hike to Malpaso Beach

The best things in life often require a little more effort. The same goes for the beaches of Sayulita. If you're looking for some of the best beaches in the area while hiking in Sayulita, head to Malpaso Beach.

Malpaso Beach is one of the wildest and most pristine beaches in the area. It is located north of Sayulita, between Sayulita and San Pancho. Getting there isn't easy (nor is it difficult).

If you make the effort to get there, you'll probably have it all to yourself.

- To get to Playa Malpaso, go to Sayulita Main Beach and continue walking north past all the hotels and resorts.
- Once you reach the end of the trail, take the road that leads over the headland and into the jungle.
- On the other side is Malpaso Beach, where you can spend the day playing in the waves and enjoying the pristine nature.

There are no services there,So please bring everything you need for the day. Water, drinks, snacks, fruit, towels, etc.

Eat Authentic Mexican Food

Make the most of your stay in Mexico with Sayulita's ubiquitous tacos, grilled fish and seafood, tostadas and enchiladas can do. Everyone enjoys great authentic food.

Tacos are the most popular food there. Restaurants and food stalls all serve popular classics. There are plenty of other dishes to try, including seafood tostadas, grilled seafood, and mole (though you'll have to drive to Oaxaca for the best mole).

Hike Monkey Mountain Sayulita

Just south of Sayulita is a small mountain or hill called Monkey Mountain.

Sayulita's Monkey Mountain Hike is perfect for those who want to add a little Sayulita hiking to their trip, or for those who want to get out of town and explore a little more.

Although not the best hike ever, the views from the top of the surrounding jungle and ocean are amazing. The best time to climb is sunset or prime time. Be sure to bring a headlamp to light your way home.

If you visit Sayulita during whale watching season (December to March), keep an eye out for whales. You will need to take a car or taxi to reach the starting point of the hike.Taxi drivers know the place. Just say "Cerro del Mono" and they will take you to the starting point.

Yoga Practice

Sayulita's surrounding landscape is full of opportunities for those dedicated to the practice of yoga - year-round classes, drop-ins, and yoga retreats. Many yoga teachers visit Sayulita each year, but some of the city's best and most recommended teachers have long been based in Sayulita. Vinyasa, hatha and restorative yoga are offered at all of the city's shalas, but you can also find acroyoga and less traditional SUP yoga classes.

5

Indulging Your Senses

A Culinary Adventure

Sayulita's attractions aren't just limited to beaches and sunsets. It also extends to its vibrant culinary scene, fresh seafood, authentic Mexican flavors, and an astonishingly rich tapestry of vegetarian and vegan cuisine. So, get ready to whet your appetite and tantalize your taste buds.

Sea to Fork

Fresh Seafood Feast Enjoy seafood at Sayulita's waterfront restaurant. Enjoy juicy grilled fish tacos packed with flavor and freshness while watching the sunset on the horizon. Dive into a piping hot bowl of caldo de Pescado, a hearty fish soup prepared with local vegetables and spices.

Don't miss the signature ceviche, a flavorful and refreshing seafood salad perfect for a light lunch or appetizer. Each bite pays homage to the ocean's bounty, lovingly prepared and seasoned with Sayulita saltiness.

Location

Barracuda Sayulita: Known for its fresh game and ocean views.

El Pescador Poke Bar: Create your own Poke Bowl using carefully selected fresh ingredients.

Mariscos Puerto Vallarta: Authentic seafood dishes with a local twist.

Pozole

Embark on a culinary journey through the rich flavors of Mexico. "al pastor" tacos, marinated pork cooked on a vertical spit and served with fresh pineapple salsa.

Enjoy a comforting bowl of pozole, a slow-cooked stew of pork or chicken with hominy. Be sure to try the traditional "mole. It is a complex and flavorful sauce that comes in a variety of regional styles, each with unique spices and ingredients. Every bite is connected to the traditions of Mexican cuisine, passed down through generations, and served with a warm smile.

Location

La Rústica: A must for traditional Mexican cuisine with a modern twist.

Mary's Traditional Mexican Cuisine: Authentic taste and generous portions.

El Itacate: A local favorite known for delicious and affordable tacos.

Vegetarian and Vegan Delicacies

Sayulita is not just for seafood lovers and meat eaters.Vegetarians and vegans will love it, The city has an incredible variety of delicious and creative plant-based options. Filled with fresh fruit and granola, these colorful acai bowls are the perfect healthy breakfast.

Enjoy a hearty veggie burger bursting with flavor and texture, made with black beans, sweet potatoes, and portobello mushrooms. Don't miss the bright tinga, made from jackfruit, a meat substitute simmered in a smoky chipotle sauce.

Every bite is a testament to Sayulita's culinary ingenuity and creativity, proving that plant-based meals can be just as filling and delicious.

Location

 Organi-k: A paradise for health-conscious foodies with smoothies, salads, and vegan bowls.

Yambak: Serving delicious and innovative vegetarian and vegan tacos.

The Green Room: A cafe serving healthy breakfast and lunch options, including vegetarian and vegan options.

Sayulita's vibrant spirit extends beyond its sunny beaches and busy streets. The culinary scene is a kaleidoscope of flavors catering to every taste and mood. Whether you're looking for a pick-me-up in the morning, a healthy lunch break, or a romantic dinner under the stars, Sayulita has you covered.

Cafe and Juice Bar

Sayulita Coffee: This local favorite offers delicious coffee, pastries, and a lively atmosphere to fuel your day. (Avenida Revolución)

Bruja Café & Boutique: Enjoy specialty coffee, homemade granola, and healthy smoothies in a charming setting. (Calle Delfines)

The Green Room: Enjoy fresh juices, smoothies, and healthy breakfast bowls with a focus on sustainability. (Calle Marlin)

The Real Coconut: Enjoy refreshing coconut water, acai bowls, and smoothies made with real ingredients. (Avenida Revolución)

Sayulita's cafes and juice bars are more than just places to grab a drink. These are social spaces where locals and visitors gather, share stories, and absorb the energy of the city. Start your day with a frothy latte and crispy croissant, enjoy a protein smoothie after your morning workout, or rejuvenate with a refreshing juice after a stroll around town.

Healthy Options

Organi-k: This health paradise features vegetarian and vegan dishes, salads, and smoothies. (Avenida Revolución)

Yambak: Enjoy innovative vegetarian and vegan tacos made with fresh, local ingredients. (Calle Marlin)

Bowls & More: Create your own acai bowl with a variety of toppings and healthy snacks. (Marlin Street)

Sayulita Farmers Market: Stock up on fresh fruits, vegetables, and local produce at the lively market on Fridays. (Calle Gaviotas)

Sayulita offers a wide range of nutritious and delicious options for health-conscious travelers. From energizing breakfast bowls to hearty salads and creative vegan dishes, there's something to suit every taste and nourish your body.

Rooftop Restaurant

Hippie-chic Sayulita: Enjoy delicious Mexican food and stunning ocean views from this rooftop restaurant. (Calle Marlin)

Iguana Rooftop Bar & Grill: Enjoy fresh seafood, cocktails, and panoramic city and ocean views. (Calle Marlin)

The Roof at Hotelito Sayulita: Enjoy Italian cuisine and breathtaking sunsets from this intimate rooftop terrace. (Calle Delfines)

For a truly unforgettable dining experience, Sayulita's rooftop restaurant offers a unique combination of delicious food, breathtaking views, and a romantic atmosphere. Imagine sipping cocktails, enjoying a gourmet meal under the stars, and soaking up the gentle sea breeze as the sun dips below the horizon.

Intimate Restaurant

La Bahia: Enjoy a romantic evening with a candlelit atmosphere, fresh seafood, and live music at this beachfront restaurant (Avenida Revolución)

Don Felipe: Enjoy authentic Mexican cuisine in a charming courtyard setting, perfect for special occasions. (Calle María Teresa)

Los Cocos: Enjoy Italian cuisine and a cozy atmosphere with sea views. Perfect for a romantic dinner. (Calle Delfines)

Nightlife Scene

Imagine enjoying a delicious meal with your loved ones, surrounded by soft lighting, gentle music, and the warm glow of candles. Whether you prefer a beachfront location or a charming courtyard, Sayulita offers the perfect setting to create lasting memories with your special someone.

Even as the sun disappears below the horizon, Sayulita's vibrant spirit remains undiminished. The city is a symphony of laughter, music, and dance, inviting you to the rhythm of nightlife. Grab your dancing shoes, let down your inhibitions, and get ready to experience the magic of Sayulita after sunset.

Lively Bar

La Patrona Bar & Grill: This lively bar transforms into a stage for energetic folklore dance shows on select nights, a glimpse into Mexican culture. (Marlin Street)

Barracuda Sayulita: Enjoy a relaxed atmosphere with ocean views, refreshing cocktails, and live music on select nights. (Calle Marlin)

Sayulita Pub: This classic pub offers a large selection of beers, live sports on TV, and a friendly atmosphere where you can mingle with locals and fellow travelers.(Calle Revolución)

Atico Rooftop Bar: Listen to a DJ, sip a handcrafted cocktail from this rooftop bar, and take in stunning sunset views. (Calle María Teresa)

Sayulitas Bar offers something for every mood. Whether you're looking for a relaxed atmosphere with live music and conversation, a lively atmosphere with dancing and laughter, or a rooftop terrace with great views and cocktails.

Live Music

The Roof at Hotelito Sayulita: Enjoy live musical performances by local artists on our cozy rooftop terrace overlooking the ocean (Calle Delfines)

La Peña Sayulita: Immerse yourself in the soulful sounds of Mexican folk music at this traditional bar with live performances. (Calle María Teresa)

El Barrilito: Move your feet, listen to the sounds of reggae, and enjoy the relaxed atmosphere with friendly locals. (Calle Revolución)

Sayulita Farmers Market: Stroll through the lively market on Fridays and experience live music by local groups. (Calle Gaviotas)

Dancing

Mama Sayulita: This beach club features live music, DJ beats, and a lively dance floor late into the night. (Avenida Revolución)

Mandala Sayulita: This outdoor club offers international DJs, live music events, and a lively dance floor under the stars. (Calle Delfines)

Coco's Beach Club: Dance on the moonlit beach to live music and DJ sets at this popular spot, especially during the Full Moon Party. (Avenida del Palmar)

Outdoor Beach Party: Impromptu beach parties are held on the shores of Sayulita all year round, offering a unique opportunity to dance with locals and tourists under the stars. (Location varies)

Swing your hips under the stars, feel the sand between your toes, and let the rhythm of the music guide you.These experiences are more than just dances. They are a celebration of life, community, and magic in Sayulita after sunset.

Remember

- Be respectful to locals and other guests.

- Keep noise levels appropriate and be aware of your surroundings.
- Comfortable, casual clothing.
- Sayulita's nightlife is laid-back, so ditch your fancy dresses and soak up the beach vibe.
- Pace yourself and stay hydrated.
- The fun can last a long time, so drink responsibly and stay safe.

Shopping Spree

Beach essentials

Sayulita Surf Shop: Get ready for your next ocean adventure with surfboards, wetsuits, and beach accessories. (Avenida Revolución)

Sun and Sea: Here you'll find everything you need for a day at the beach, from sunscreen and hats to towels and umbrellas. (Calle Marlin)

Olas Atlas: Rent a surfboard, stand-up paddleboard, or kayak and explore the coast at your own pace. (Avenida Revolución)

From sarongs to sunglasses, beach essentials are at your fingertips in Sayulita, so you're ready to soak up the sun and enjoy the magic of the ocean.

Handmade Crafts

Arte Sayulita: Discover unique creations by local artisans, including jewelry, sculptures, and paintings, infused with the city's artistic spirit. (Calle Delfines)

Cooperativa Sayulita: Support your local community by purchasing handmade souvenirs made from sustainable materials like recycled glass and coconut shells. (Calle Marlin)

More than just souvenirs, these handcrafted items are tangible parts of Sayulita's soul, each imbued with the story and skill of the artisans who created it.

Unique Clothing and Jewelry

Boho Chic Sayulita: Find flowy dresses, beach cover-ups, and locally designed swimwear to add to your wardrobe Add some bohemian flair. (Calle Marlin)

Sayulita Surfwear: Find surfer-inspired clothing, accessories, and locally designed jewelry perfect to express your love of the ocean (Avenida Revolución)

Soluna: Browse our selection of unique clothing, jewelry, and accessories made by independent designers and local artisans. (Calle Delfines)

Beyond Shopping

Shopping in Sayulita is about more than just buying products. It's about engaging with the local community, valuing their skills, and bringing back some of the city's unique spirit.

Contact the craftsmen, listen to their stories, and negotiate with a smile. Let your purchases be a reminder of the warmth, color, and artistry that makes Sayulita special.

Sayulita is waiting with open arms for hidden treasure to be discovered. So, set your wanderlust free, set your curiosity free, and be enchanted by the magic that lies beyond the beach.

Art Market and Craft Stalls

Location: The streets of Sayulita come alive with a vibrant art market and craft stalls, creating a colorful tapestry of creativity throughout the city. These markets and stalls are scattered in the main square, along the promenade, and in hidden corners of Sayulita.

Art Market

Immerse yourself in Sayulita's vibrant art scene by exploring the vibrant Art Market, where local artists and artisans showcase their talents and sell their work.

These markets often display artwork in a variety of styles, from traditional Mexican folk art to modern, avant-garde pieces, including paintings, sculptures, pottery, and textiles.

Discover unique works of art and meet the artists behind them by strolling through market stalls such as the Mercado del Pueblo, held on Fridays in the main plaza.

Enjoy live music, street performances, and a festive atmosphere while browsing colorful exhibits and finding unique souvenirs to take home.

Craft Stalls

In addition to the organized art market, Sayulita has numerous craft stalls located throughout the city where local artisans sell their handmade items. These stalls can be found along the streets and lanes of Sayulita, selling everything from handmade jewelry and textiles to wood carvings and leather goods.

Explore Calle Revolucion and Calle Delfin to discover hidden gems hidden in charming alleyways and courtyards. There you can admire the craftsmanship of Sayulita's talented artisans and purchase unique and authentic treasures.

Sustainable and Eco-Friendly Products

Many stores and boutiques offer a wide range of sustainable and eco-friendly products. These products can be found in various locations around the city, including eco-friendly stores, organic markets, and sustainable boutiques.

Eco-Friendly Stores

Sayulita is home to a growing number of eco-friendly stores dedicated to promoting sustainable lifestyles and eco-friendly products. These stores offer a wide selection of eco-friendly products, including reusable products, biodegradable household products, and organic skin care and beauty products.

Look for stores like Mi Esperanza on Calle Marlin that offer a selection of sustainable products like bamboo toothbrushes, stainless steel straws, and natural sunscreen.

Whether you're shopping for yourself or looking for eco-friendly gifts for your home, Sayulita's eco-friendly stores offer a guilt-free shopping experience that supports sustainability and protecting the environment.

Organic Market

Sayulita's Organic Market is a treasure trove of local, organic, and sustainable products, including fresh produce, artisan foods, and handmade crafts. These markets often have vendors who emphasize sustainable farming, ethical production methods, and fair trade principles.

Visit markets like the Mercado del Pueblo, held on Fridays in the main plaza, to buy organic fruits and vegetables, artisan cheeses and breads, and artisan goods made with care and respect for the environment.

By supporting these organic markets, you can enjoy fresh, healthy produce while contributing to the conservation of Sayulita's natural resources and the well-being of the local community.

6

Practical Information

Essential Sayulita

Sayulita, Mexico, invites guests from all over the world, and so does its budgetary framework. Here's what you wish to know almost money trade and ATMs to guarantee your trip is smooth cruising:

Official Money: Mexican Peso (MXN),Typically the official money of Mexico, and the one you'll utilize for most buys in Sayulita.

Currency Exchange:

Trading USD for MXN: You'll trade your US dollars (USD) for pesos at different areas in Sayulita, counting:

Casas de Cambio: These are committed money trade booths found all through town. Compare rates some time recently choosing one.

Banks: Intercam Bank is the as it were bank in Sayulita, but others are available in adjacent Bucerias.

Lodgings: Numerous lodgings offer money trade administrations, but rates might not be the finest.

Tips for Currency Exchange

Compare rates: Do not fair go to the primary put you see. Check rates at numerous areas to induce the finest bargain.

Inquire around expenses: A few places charge covered up expenses for trading cash, so be beyond any doubt to inquire forthright.

Consider utilizing ATMs: Frequently, utilizing an ATM with a charge card with no outside exchange expenses is the foremost cost-effective way to urge pesos.

ATMs

ATMs are promptly accessible in Sayulita, both at Intercam Bank and at different comfort stores and eateries. Be mindful of potential fees charged by your bank and the ATM administrator. Seek for ATMs with the Visa Furthermore or Mastercard Cirrus symbol, as they may have lower expenses.

Utilize ATMs in well-lit, open regions and dodge utilizing them at night. Be watchful and keep your Stick private.

Credit Cards

Numerous businesses in Sayulita accept major credit cards, but be mindful that a few may charge remote exchange expenses.

Travel Debit Cards

Consider getting a travel charge card with no foreign transaction expenses for helpful and cost-effective spending.

Keep in Mind That

- Having a few pesos on hand after you arrive is supportive for taxis, tipping, and little buys.
- A great technique is to utilize a combination of cash (pesos) and credit/debit cards for flexibility and security.
- By understanding your alternatives and taking safeguards, you'll be able guarantee your money woes are non-existent amid your Sayulita experience.
- Download a cash converter app to your phone for simple on-the-go calculations.

Staying Connected

Staying connected while visiting Sayulita is basic for keeping in touch with cherished ones, sharing your enterprises on social media, and getting to imperative data. Luckily, Sayulita offers different choices for Wi-Fi and phone administrations to keep you associated all through your remain.

Wi-Fi

Housing

Numerous lodgings, inns, and excursion rentals in Sayulita offer complimentary Wi-Fi to their visitors. Sometime recently booking your settlement, check whether Wi-Fi is included and ask approximately the quality and unwavering quality of the association.

Cafés and Eateries

Various cafés, eateries, and bars in Sayulita give free Wi-Fi to benefactors . Appreciate a glass of coffee or a tasty supper while catching up on emails or browsing the net at one of Sayulita's cozy foundations.

Open Hotspots

Sayulita's primary square and shoreline zones may have open Wi-Fi hotspots accessible for guests. Keep an eye out for signs showing Wi-Fi accessibility in open zones, and take advantage of these helpful spots to remain associated on the go.

Neighborhood SIM Cards

Buy a SIM Card

For travelers remaining in Sayulita for an amplified period or those who require a consistent network, acquiring a nearby SIM card could be a helpful choice. SIM cards can be acquired from different versatile arrange suppliers, such as Telcel, Movistar, and AT&T, at comfort stores, drug stores, or official stores in Sayulita.

Top-Up Credit

After purchasing a SIM card, you'll have to beat up your credit to actuate an information arrangement and make calls or send writings. Top-up credit can be obtained from comfort stores, general stores, and authorized retailers all through Sayulita.

Mobile Data Packages

network providers in Sayulita offer a range of information bundles to suit distinctive utilization needs and budgets. Choose an information bundle that gives adequate information stipend for your planning utilization, whether it's browsing the net, gushing substance, or utilizing social media.

Mobile Coverage

While Mobile Coverage in Sayulita is generally great, the scope may shift depending on your area inside the town and the organized supplier you select. Be beyond any doubt that inaccessible or disconnected zones, such as certain shorelines or wilderness trails, may have constrained or no Mobile Coverage.

By taking advantage of Wi-Fi hotspots, nearby SIM cards, and portable information bundles, you'll be able to remain associated with and appreciate a consistent travel encounter while investigating the charming town of Sayulita.

Safety and Security Tips

Common Sense Precautions

Sayulita, like any tourist destination, requests caution and common sense from visitors to ensure a safe and enjoyable experience.

Here are some common sense precautions to stay safe during your stay in Sayulita:

Always Stay Alert: Keep your belongings safe and aware of your surroundings, especially in crowded areas like markets and beaches.

Precautions for Night Use: Although Sayulita is generally safe, it is recommended that you do not walk alone in dimly lit or secluded areas at night. Drive on well-lit roads and travel in groups if possible.

Avoid Excessive Drinking: Drink responsibly and watch your alcohol intake, especially when exploring nightlife. Excessive drinking can impair your judgment and make you more susceptible to accidents and theft.

Sun Protection: Sayulita's sunny climate means you'll be spending a lot of time outdoors. So to avoid sunburn and heatstroke, remember to wear sunscreen, stay hydrated, and seek shade during the hottest parts of the day.

Beware of Scams: Be wary of street vendors, especially those selling counterfeit goods or offering deals that seem too good to be true. To avoid becoming a victim of fraud, use trusted stores and companies.

Know your Emergency Contacts: Know your local emergency contacts, including numbers for the police, medical services, and your country's embassy or consulate.

Follow Beach Safety Guidelines: Be aware of warning signs and flags on the beach that indicate possible hazards, such as strong currents or dangerous marine life.

Travel with Caution: If you rent a car or use public transport, please drive safely and obey traffic laws. Be careful when crossing roads, especially in areas with heavy traffic.

Local Customs and Etiquette Location: Sayulita is a welcoming and friendly city, but to ensure positive interactions with residents and other visitors, please respect local customs and etiquette.

 Greetings: When meeting someone for the first time, a friendly Hola (hello) or Buenos dias (good morning) is sufficient.

Handshakes are common in formal settings, but hugs and kisses on the cheek are more common among friends and acquaintances.

Politeness: Politeness is very important in Mexican culture. So when making a request or getting help, remember to say por favor (please) and gracias (thank you).

When addressing elderly people or strangers, it is appropriate to use usted (the formal form of you).

Appropriate Attire: Sayulita has a relaxed atmosphere, but it is important to dress modestly when visiting churches and other religious sites to respect local customs. It's fine to wear beachwear at the beach, but consider covering up while eating or walking around town.

Tipping: Tipping is common in Mexico, especially in the service sector. It is customary to leave a tip of around 10-15% in restaurants, bars, and other services such as taxis and tour guides.

Respect Cultural Sites: When visiting cultural or religious sites, such as churches or archaeological sites, respect the sanctity of the site by observing all posted rules and regulations.

Be Patient: Mexican culture values a relaxed rhythm of life. So be prepared for things to move more slowly than before. Practice patience and flexibility, especially when it comes to waiting in lines and dealing with delays.

Additional Resources

Embarking on a Sayulita adventure requires more than just packing your swimsuit and developing your wanderlust.To truly discover this city's hidden gems, cultural nuances, and off-the-beaten-path experiences, your trusty digital girlfriend companion is essential.

Hotel Booking:

Booking.com: A popular platform with a wide range of hotels, hostels, and vacation rentals in Sayulita.

Expedia: Another major player offering hotels, flights, and vacation packages.

Airbnb: Ideal for finding unique apartments, villas, and private homes for a more local experience.

Website

Sayulita Life : https://www.sayulitalife.com/

This comprehensive website is your one-stop-shop for all things Sayulita, including an event calendar, business directory, surf reports, and insight into local culture, food, and activities. From hidden waterfalls to the best taco stands, Sayulita Life has you covered.

Sayulita Surf Report :https://www.surfline.com/surfreport/sayulita/5842042 04e65fad6a77091fa)

This website will help you get out on the water at the perfect time and conditions. It provides detailed surf reports, live cameras, and weather forecasts for Sayulita Beach.

Blog

GringAdventures: (https: //gringajourneys.com/)

Follow the adventures of expats Kristen and Siya as they explore Sayulita and beyond. Their blog is filled with stunning photography, detailed travel guides, and honest reviews of restaurants, activities, and hidden gems, offering her a unique perspective on her life in Sayulita.

App

Sayulita Life App: https://www.sayulitalife.com/

Enjoy this handy app with interactive maps, business listings, event updates, and offline access to important information. This is your pocket guide to navigating the streets and hidden gems of Sayulita.

Surf in Mexico: https://www.wavetribe.com/blogs/surf-travel/the-only-gui de-to-surfing-in-mexico-you-ll-ever-need

Whether you're a seasoned surfer or a curious beginner, this app provides tidal charts, swell forecasts, and surf spot reviews specific to Sayulita and the surrounding area. Plan your surfing sessions with confidence and discover new waves to conquer.

XE Currency Converter: https://www.xe.com/apps/

Avoid tourist traps and trade like a pro with this currency converter app. Instantly convert Pesos to your home currency to get the best deals and ensure you make informed financial decisions while traveling.

To help you plan your trip and get around the city easily, here's a comprehensive guide with maps and transportation information:

Maps

Online Maps: Explore online before your trip Please familiarize yourself with Sayulita's location using maps and satellite images. Websites and apps like Google Maps and MapQuest provide detailed maps of Sayulita, including streets, landmarks, points of interest, and more.

Printed Map: When you arrive in Sayulita, pick up a printed map from your accommodation, tourist information center, or local shops and establishments. These maps often highlight popular attractions, beaches, and restaurants, making it easy to get around the city on foot or by bike.

Transportation

Walking: Sayulita's compact size and pedestrian-friendly streets make it a great city for walking. Enjoy Sayulita's laid-back atmosphere by wandering its cobblestone streets, strolling through its main square, and strolling to the beach.

Golf Cart: Renting a golf cart is a popular and convenient way to get around Sayulita, especially when exploring nearby beaches and attractions. There are golf cart rental agencies throughout the city that offer hourly, daily, and weekly rentals.

Bike: Rent a bike and cycle around Sayulita's charming streets and beautiful coastline. Many accommodations offer bicycle rental. There are also rental shops throughout the city where you can rent a variety of bicycles, including cruisers and mountain bikes.

Taxis: Sayulita has a fleet of taxis suitable for short trips around the city or to nearby destinations. Taxis can be picked up on the street or found at taxi stands located in prominent areas of Sayulita, such as the main square or the beach.

Public Transportation: Sayulita offers easy access to surrounding towns and attractions using public transportation, including buses and minibusses known as "colectivos". These shared vehicles operate on set routes and schedules, making them a cost-effective option for exploring the area.

Rental Car: If you plan to explore the area beyond Sayulita at your own pace, consider renting a car from a rental car company in town or at the nearby Puerto Vallarta Airport.

Transportation Interchange

Puerto Vallarta Airport: Sayulita is located approximately 40 kilometers (25 miles) north of Puerto Vallarta International Airport (PVR). Many tourists arrive in Puerto Vallarta by plane and then travel to Sayulita by shuttle, taxi, rental car, or public transportation.

Bus Stop: Sayulita does not have a bus terminal, but nearby cities such as Puerto Vallarta and Bucerias have central bus stops, allowing you to reach Sayulita via local buses or collectivos.

Road Signs: Look for road signs and landmarks to help you navigate the streets of Sayulita. These are arranged in a grid with streets numbered from east to west (calles) and streets numbered from north to south (Avenida).

Packing Essentials

Expectations are high as you begin your journey to Sayulita, a picturesque beach town on Mexico's Pacific coast. Come explore its sandy beaches, lively streets, and laid-back atmosphere. But before you set off on your adventure, there's one more important task.

As you pack your bags, imagine the sun-drenched days ahead and the countless experiences that await you in this tropical paradise. First of all, dress lightly, opting for airy tops, comfortable shorts, and flowing summer dresses.

Sayulita's warm climate requires practical and stylish clothing to stay cool as you stroll the city's cobblestone streets or relax on the sun-drenched beaches. Throw on your swimsuit and board shorts and you'll know that water adventures await just beyond the shore.

Next, let's turn to sunscreen, which is essential for those days soaking up the bright Sayulita sun. Pack your favorite sun hat and sunglasses to keep your face out of the shade while you enjoy the coastal views.

High SPF sunscreen is a must on your packing list, as is soothing aloe vera gel in case you get an unexpected sunburn. With several days of water activities ahead of you, you want to pack your snorkeling gear and explore a vibrant underwater world teeming with marine life.

Surfboards and boogie boards are essential for catching waves and riding swells, while umbrellas provide relief from the midday sun when you're having a leisurely picnic by the seaside.

In addition to your fun-in-the-sun essentials, make sure you have space in your luggage for everyday essentials. A lightweight backpack will always be your companion, perfect for carrying essentials like a reusable water bottle, travel-sized hand sanitizer, and a portable power bank to charge your devices on the go.

Health and safety comes first. Therefore, prepare a basic first aid kit with bandages, painkillers, and any necessary prescription medications.

Sayulita is ready for your adventure and has everything you need for an unforgettable journey. From sandy beaches to bustling markets, this charming coastal paradise promises new discoveries and unforgettable experiences every day.

Once you've completed your packing list, you'll be ready to enjoy every moment and create precious memories that will last a lifetime.

Tour Guides Contact

Surfing

Sayulita Surf School: Learn to catch waves from the pros at Sayulita Surf School, known for its experienced instructors and fun atmosphere. They offer group and private lessons for all skill levels, so you'll be progressing like a local in no time.

   Contact: +52 (322) 223-0018

La Palapa Surf School

Another great option for surfing lessons is La Palapa Surf School. Choose from a variety of packages, including multi-day courses and surf camps. Additionally, the teachers are very friendly and patient and will help you have fun while learning.

   Contact: +52 (322) 223-0212

Stand-Up Paddleboarding

SUP Sayulita

SUP Explore Sayulita's coast and turquoise waters on a Sayulita stand-up paddleboard. They offer tours to suit all levels, from beginner's courses to eco-tours through hidden beaches and wildlife habitats.

  Contact: +52 (322) 223-0023

IslaPaddle

For a unique SUP experience, check out IslaPaddle. They offer tours to Isabel Island, a small island off the coast of Sayulita. It's a great way to explore the area and enjoy snorkeling and swimming in the crystal-clear waters.

  Contact: +52 (322) 223-0321

Yoga

Yoga Loft Sayulita

Start your day with a relaxing yoga class at Yoga Loft Sayulita. They offer a variety of classes, from Vinyasa and Hatha to Yin and Restorative. There is also a beautiful rooftop terrace with great views of the city and sea.

  Contact: +52 (322) 223-0412

Zipline

Canopy Tours Sayulita

Soar above the treetops on a zipline adventure at Canopy Tours Sayulita. This exciting tour takes you on a thrilling ride through the jungle with breathtaking mountain and ocean views.

Contact: +52 (322) 223-0618

Pacific Adventure Park

Get your adrenaline pumping at Pacific Adventure Park, which features a variety of ziplines, suspension bridges, and rappelling challenges. A perfect activity for families or groups of friends.

Contact: +52 (322) 223-0719

Other Tours

Sayulita Food Tours

Go on a delicious culinary adventure with Sayulita Food Tours. On this tour, you'll visit some of the best local restaurants and shops, taste traditional Mexican cuisine, and learn about the city's culture.

Important Emergency Numbers and Contact Addresses

But even in paradise, it's always a good idea to have a safety net at hand. So let's tackle some important emergency numbers and contact addresses and turn them from boring doodles to ones that protect your peace of mind:

Medical Emergencies

Ambulance

If you need Maracas for medical assistance, please dial 22- 35-00. Pressing this number will take you directly to Sayulita General Hospital, home to knights in bright white coats.

Red Cross Ambulance: For alternative medicine tango, dial 22-21-20 to connect to Red Cross Ambulance. They will take you to the hospital immediately.

Ameri-Med Hospital: Feeling unwell? This private hospital is staffed by bilingual physicians and offers a wide range of treatments. Think of it as a medical mariachi band that will bring you back to health. Please contact them at 22-38-38-38.

Security and Emergencies

 City Police: If you are having trouble while on vacation, please dial 22-38-38-34. Friendly police officers will keep you on your toes, ensuring your safety and solving any problems with Mexican hospitality.

Tourist Police: Need assistance with a problem pertaining to tourists or are you lost? Please inquire about the Tourist Police by calling 22-38-38-34. They will be your multilingual guides, guiding you through every circumstance with a smile.

Consulate Puerto Vallarta: Call (322) 226-8777 to reach the US Consulate in Puerto Vallarta if you're a US citizen in need of assistance. They will be your partners in the diplomatic dance, providing help and direction when needed.

Few Key Spanish Phrases

While English is widely spoken in tourist areas, learning a few key Spanish phrases will unlock deeper connections and enrich your experience.

Greetings and Essentials

- **Hola:** Hello (universal greeting)
- **Buenos días/tardes/noches:** Good morning/afternoon/evening (time-specific greetings)
- **Cómo estás/están?:** How are you/you all? (informal)
- **Habla inglés?:** Do you speak English?
- **Gracias:** Thank you
- **De nada:** You're welcome
- **Por favor:** Please
- **Lo siento:** I'm sorry
- **No entiendo:** I don't understand

Restaurant and Shopping

- **Cuánto cuesta?:** How much does this cost?
- **Me gustaría...:** I would like...
- **Tiene...?:** Do you have...?
- **Una cerveza, por favor:** One beer, please
- **Puedo pagar con tarjeta?:** Can I pay with a card?

Directions and Getting Around

- **Dónde está...?:** Where is...?
- **A cuánto queda...?:** How far is it to...?
- **Derecho/izquierda?:** Right/left?
- **Recto?:** Straight ahead?

- **Cuánto dura el viaje?:** How long does the trip take?
- **Cuánto me cobra?:** How much do you charge?

Cultural Gems

- Me puede recomendar...? Can you recommend...? (restaurants, activities)
- Qué hay de interesante para ver?: What is interesting to see here?
- Me gusta...: I like...
- Qué hermoso/a: How beautiful!
- Muchas gracias: Thank you very much

Made in the USA
Columbia, SC
17 December 2024

49631561R00043